BUSINESS

BOOSTER TODAY MAGAZINE

VOL. 1 | NO. 2 | JUNE 2018

DAVID FABRICIUS

THE MOVERS AND SHAKERS

Feature

SABINE ZETTL

CONTENTS

IMPRESS

PUBLISHER & EDITOR IN CHIEF

Christian Bartsch (Leading Author)

FEATURE EDITOR & VP

Sue Baumgaertner-Bartsch

ADVISING EDITOR

Udo Bartsch

VIP PHOTOGRAPHY

Gábor Dobos

VIP STYLING & MAKEUP

Aldrin-David Verburgt

GRAPHICS & WEBDESIGN

Mizanur Rahman

ISBN-13:

978-3-947256-07-5

PUBLISHED BY

ACATO GmbH

PUBLICATION DATE

24.06.2018

PUBLICATION SERIES INFO

June 2018 No. 2

PARTNERS

Hazel Herrington

Orsi Beata Nagy

Shadeska Nicolina

Sylvija Popovic

John Stokoe

AMBASSADORS

Vikas Malkani
Sally Forrest

HOW TO CONTACT US

www.businessboostertoday.com

ADVERTISING & SALES

sales@businessboostertoday.com

Phone +49 89 54041070

Business Booster Today is published by ACATO GmbH, 1st. Floor, Theresienhoehe 27, 80339 Munich, Germany.

CONNECT WITH US

Read more Business Booster Today Magazine content at BusinessBoosterToday.com

Download the **Business Booster Today App** for iPhone or Android.

Like the **Business Booster Today Magazine on Facebook** for the latest news, photos, videos and exclusive online content.

Follow **@mybbtmagazine** on Twitter and keep informed on breaking news and busines trends.

View stories and photos on Instagram and get a backstage insight. Follow us at **businessboostertoday**

Make connections with fellow entrepreneurs and business people in our community at businessboostertoday.com

FOUNDERS CORNER

The world of business keeps rolling our great opportunities to gain success by focusing on an international business model.

By Sue Baumgärtner-Bartsch & Christian Bartsch

The business world keeps changing as technology, trends and global events influence the performance of established brands. The turbulences also affect rising starts and those who are considering leaving their corporate job in order to start their own business.

The reality of entrepreneurial life is that risks will always be there to create an uncertainty. Success is based on the determination that drives an innovative entrepreneur.

Entrepreneurs who are just embarking on their journey to take their business idea to a sustainable enterprise will feel this uncertainty. Many people who do not belief in their ability to achieve success will try to lure them away from their success. These negative people will try to plant doubt into their minds. It will take a

considerable amount of courage to continue on that path.

Nevertheless, there is one vital factor that makes successful entrepreneurs reach their goals: they are coachable.

You should not listen to the negative people and the unsuccessful people who want to destroy your success. You need to listen to the experienced and successful people. You need to have a coach.

The most successful people surround themselves with other successful

entrepreneurs and bounce topics of their coaches. The worlds #1 Wealth coach J.T. Foxx has more than 8 coaches to bounce of ideas and difficult decisions.

Coaching makes millionaires by the advice and guidance they receive. It is up to the entrepreneur to develop and implement strategies to reach the desired outcomes.

With this edition of the Business Booster Today Magazine we are show casing successful entrepreneurs and providing a platform to share knowledge. We want to feature the shakers and movers of the business world.

EDITORIAL TEAM

Christian Bartsch (Publisher, Editor in Chief)

Christian is a speaker and digital forensics expert in niche areas. His company focuses on educating people on how to optimize their sales and customer lifecycle. Due to his special expertise, he guides businesses along the path to protecting trade secrets in the corporate environment.

Sue Baumgärtner-Bartsch (Lead Editor, VP, MC)

Sue is a serial entrepreneur, Peak Potential coach, mother, and wife who has lived and worked on 3 continents. She has worked as an auditor and consultant with companies on a global scale for 10+ years before starting her own business.

Orsi Beata Nagy

Hungary & Eastern Europe Editor

Hazel Herrington

Africa Editor

Silvija Popovic

Croatia Editor

John Stokoe

Property Editor

Gábor Dobos

VIP Photographer

Shadeska Nicolina

Curacao & Netherlands Editor

Udo Bartsch

Export & Photo-Optic Editor

Aldrin-David Verburgt

VIP Stylist

EDITOR OF THE EDITION

Orsi Beata Nagy (Eastern EU Editor & Regional Partner)

As a business strategist, she has one goal – to make your organization run more efficiently, saving you and your company time and money. She has over 8+ years of experience in setting up business systems and processes for UK's main transport national, international companies, small businesses, and entrepreneurs.

BRANDING EXPOSURE COACHES

The aura of authenticity and credibility grows by putting the best form of visual elements out to the world. The first impression is like the beauty of diamonds.

Gábor Dobos (VIP Photographer)

Gábor is a well-known global brand builder who creates fantastic images and films for entrepreneurs, companies, global organizations and A-List celebrities. He believes that professional images and films give you a higher brand credibility. He travels around to world for his clients to capture their powerful moments which are unrepeatable.

Aldrin-David Verburgt (VIP Stylist)

Aldrin-David is a well-known VIP stylist for entrepreneurs and business people around the world, including Hollywood celebrities like Charlie Sheen. He pays attention to not only your look but your overall appearance and brand. His mission is to maximize your image for success, so you not only look the part but act the part of success to win the deal.

CRISTINA STAVENSKI

Swiss entrepreneur advocating for a healthy lifestyle to prolong life

Interview by Sue Baumgärtner-Bartsch

What is your key to success?

Create value persistently + increase your relationship capital + believe in the transformational quality of your project = Changing Lives.

What you do?

The Slow Planet is the first integrated and inclusive community in the world for Slow. It aims to provide creative collaborative solutions to private entities, building rapport with the public organizations for a genuinely sustainable evolution of both – the human kind and the planet.

The broader vision of the community is to place together all the entities that produce innovative durable goods and services with their biggest supporters for an organic development of the global systems in the shortest time possible.

As the founder and the managing partner of the Slow Planet, my contribution is to build relationship capital from both private and public organizations. Our team actually helps them collaborate successfully in a capitalistic world making the innovative systems work for them, not against them.

What motivated you to launch a business?

Still nowadays with the entire technological breakthrough available worldwide, communication is the biggest issue. I am an innate communicator and decided to become the interface between the 2 main decisional structures (companies and the government) that speak different languages, even if they speak the same ethnical language. The time has come for SLOW to become faster.

Either we consider health, lifestyle, business or spirituality everything respects its cycles. We cannot influence them. The only thing we can influence is how we evolve within optimizing that cycle for the benefit of others, hence our business. If we choose to run after… we will always run the rat race. In that optic we might as well loose our financial wealth or worse – our health and family.

In order to be in syntony with our rhythm and to be able to give in the best to the people who surround us, we have to slow down, reflect on what we are doing right and what we are doing wrong, reassess the situation and get back on track faster than ever: energized with a clear mind and soul to reach for the stars. A sick mind and body will go nowhere. Beware and make sure you get the appropriate guidance in this matter, because you are the master of your own life and destiny!

If you are one of millions of people that are looking for a new way of living and doing business in a sustainable manner above generations, then the Slow Planet is THE community to give you that type of support.

Name 3 business principles that are of core value to you?

- Integrity
- Business and human ethics
- Serving People with respect and commitment

What 3 core advice principals will you give entrepreneurs that are wanting to start their own business?

- Get the best coach in your area of business and the team that shares your values and business vision (culture)
- Focus on what you are best at and delegate the rest
- Stay open to change, challenge and creative solutions implementation (instant) for the best client satisfaction of needs and desires

ALDRIN-DAVID VERBURGT

He firmly believes in the utter importance of balance in taking good care of your physique, skin and hair, whether you want to sport the natural look or totally glam.

Interviewed by Sue Baumgärtner-Bartsch

Aldrin-David started out working in the world of aesthetics by mastering the Total Art of Hair. Applying several cutting edge technical skills to create personal designed haircuts and various techniques in colouring that will emphasize depth, fullness and richness while being fashionable, is one of his trademarks.

As a colour specialist he continued to broaden his skills as a make-up artist in order to provide total value to his clients. Feeling very fortunate that he is able to do what he really likes and is passionate about, he also **loves sharing his knowledge in haircare, styling and skincare**. Guiding and <u>educating colleagues in new trends</u> or the basic/classic theory and techniques of the trade is what he has done throughout his creative career.

Aldrin-David also expanded his knowledge as an *aesthetician performing luxury skin treatments and educating people* in how to take good care of your skin to remain healthy looking and to **prevent premature aging**.

Having worked with all the international beauty brands, he believes that a combination of all his knowledge and experience in the world of aesthetics, beauty, health and presentation backed up by science, is a great way to provide value. He not only creates awareness but offers direct solutions to boost people's physical appearance.

His clients today are mostly coaches, entrepreneurs and businesspeople, and people who work in the entertainment industry. People who realize that an **"Image4Success"** is an essential part in becoming successful and to increase the chance to grow their business, to be taken seriously and above all not missing out on potential clients!

Aldrin-David focuses not only on personal styling in beauty or grooming, but also on helping his clients create professional portfolios and business branding videos to promote themselves and to bring their business to a higher level.

INTERVIEW

Give us a brief background of what you do?

My professional background is in aesthetics. I started beauty school at a young age straight out of high school. I didn't want to limit myself so continued in hair with an advanced training school. I knew from the early start that I wanted to be an all-round expert. I continued my studies to be a makeup-artist and aesthetician and a professional colourist as well.

As you can imagine creativity and applicable knowledge of colour had been a constant importance in my life and still is today.

What is the key thing you want people to know about you?

The key thing I want people to know about me is that it is important to take good care of yourself. By doing this you not only show love and respect to yourself but also to the people that you surround yourself with. That in itself is already a strong message that works for the good on an unconscious level.

What motivated you to launch your business?

The sense of more freedom, ability to grow and making your own choices instead of following a concept of someone else who's mission is their own success and not mine.

What made you seek entrepreneurial endeavours rather than traditional one?

Excitement and exploration and the bigger mental reward that comes with it.

What does success mean to you?

Being able to do the things you like to make a positive difference in the world all the while your own business is thriving, which is the engine for you to be able to do this.

Name 3 business principles that is of core value to you?

1) Giving value

2) Sharing knowledge

3) Continuous mental growth

How important is it to have a business coach & what significant role in change has your coach played in your business journey?

It makes an important difference to have a business coach, since you can reflect, share experiences, ask advice and bounce ideas with someone who already walked that path and can support and guide you to make better decisions and therefore assure you that you are on the right path.

What 3 core advice principals will you give entrepreneurs that are wanting to start their own business?

1) Do your research

2) Get support

3) Keep educating yourself

How do you overcome rejection?

Rejection is part of life and business. It's depends on different factors. A door closed now is not closed forever. Other opportunities will come, make sure you grab it!

What is the business lesson you have learned the hard way?

That you can always trust yourself but you must be willing to trust others in their expertise, because that will save you a lot of precious time.

What is your set of core values and business skills that have helped you in your career?

Creativity / Passion / Balance / Loyalty / Positivity / Open-mindedness / Courage

How important for you is work/life balance?

It's all about balance in life in order to function for a long time and in a healthy way as you should. Personal life and business are often intertwined. Therefore, balance in not a luxury it is a necessity.

How do you stay motivated and what keeps you going?

I keep myself motivated by staying in the learning curve and keep meeting other entrepreneurs so you can share experiences.

What is your favourite quote and explain why?

"Art enables us to find ourselves and lose ourselves at the same time"- by Thomas Merton. This quote is beautiful and embodies the joy of creativity and passion which is very much a part that I feel fortunate to have discovered and apply daily.

You can reach Aldrin-David at info@aldrindavid.com

SILKBRIDGE & C

ALDRIN-DAVID
HAIR/ MAKEUP
& SKIN COACH

NTREP

CONTINENTAL

GT = ?

READ PAGE 20
FOR
THE ANSWER

TO LIQUIDITY

Lower the transaction costs

By Jan Erik Horgen

It was a few minutes before 8 a.m. on one of those gray September mornings in Philadelphia, and the very ordinary looking classroom at the prestigious Wharton School of Business was already filled to the brim with students.

The classroom was buzzing with excitement as one of the **hardest finance courses** in the curriculum was about to start. Already next class, half the students in the room would have dropped out of the class.

At precisely 8 a.m. the professor stormed into the room. He was none other than the both brilliant, charismatic and notorious Jamshed Ghandi, who in addition to being a professor at **Wharton** was also a trusted advisor to three central banks and chairman of the board of a Swiss bank. Rumor had it that he was briefly expelled from Cambridge as a student for walking the rooftops in campus at night.

Upon entering the room, he would never sit down. Before even introducing himself, he had selected a suitable victim, his index finger descended from above and pointed to the student: "What is liquidity?"

The professor's cosmopolitan English was proper Cambridge English with more than a little touch of Indian accent. The student feverishly researched the deepest recesses of his mind and produced a mumbling reply. The index finger searched out another victim: "Do you agree?" An equally hesitant, but otherwise different, answer followed. The index finger reached its third victim: "Settle between them."

So, what is liquidity, and why should entrepreneurs and business boosters care? To explain the concept, the professor pointed to one of the very ordinary desk chairs in the room:

"Is this chair a liquid asset?"

What do you think? Well, it will depend on the context. Back then, every fall, at the start of the semester, students would line Locust walk, the central walkway on the campus, to buy and sell the necessities of student life.

If you at that time would walk up and down Locust Walk and marketing the chair, you would find a fair number of buyers, and the chair could be considered a relatively liquid asset. If you would try the same in February, all your potential buyers would have disappeared, and the chair would be wholly illiquid.

Was the chair any different? No, but the market had changed. So, liquidity (and say this with your best British-Indian accent) is a *continuum*. Anything you want to buy, or sell, can be placed at various points along this continuum as circumstances change. OK, that sounds like a theory, but why should I care as an entrepreneur or business booster?

You should care, because understanding what forces and circumstances shape the liquidity continuum of your business can give you a big competitive advantage.

What are some of these forces and circumstances? We have already seen one of them – the number of active and present potential buyers in the marketplace.

That's why you dragged the darn chair down to Locust Walk in the first place, to parade it in front of a large group of likely customers. Funny, sounds a lot like reasons for doing Facebook advertising… In other words, if you want your inventory to be liquid, make sure lots of potential buyers are aware of your products and that you have it in stock.

Also make sure what you have in stock actually has

AND BEYOND

... and provide added value.

potential buyers!

Having to carry the chair around is a hassle for you. Having to carry it back from Locust walk is a hassle for your potential customers. That hassle is part of the transaction costs.

If you wanted to increase demand for your chair, you could **lower the transaction cost** by promising to carry the chair to the buyer's home. Not only are you then lowering the transaction cost for your potential customer, you are also **providing added value** to your customer by doing that. Unfortunately, that comes at a cost for you: **the cost of carry**. You will need to use your business acumen and have the pulse of the market to determine if you can charge extra for providing the added value, or if the added value will simply make you the preferred desk chair supplier and close the sale.

If you carry the chair the same way the customer would have, you have not made the market more efficient, you have just transferred part of the transaction cost from buyer to seller. But what if you roller-skated over to the customer with the chair in less than half the time? Now you have **decreased the cost of transaction** and the speed of delivery and made the market more efficient. Well done!

Is more liquidity always

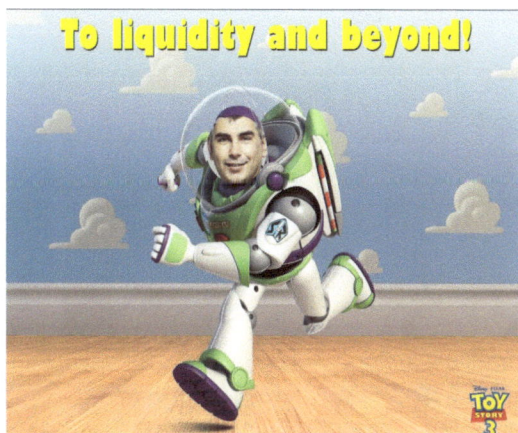

To liquidity and beyond!

better? Not if you can **get paid for illiquidity**. I am sure you have heard of the **risk-return relationship** in financial assets, where risk is the price variation, and return is your return as an investor for holding the risky asset. Fama and French are two outstanding academics, that are famous for having researched what other factors than price variation the market is willing to pay investors a premium for.

It turns out that liquidity is so valuable that investors willing to **hold illiquid assets** are paid a premium for that. Warren Buffett has made many of his best deals by having deep pockets at the right time, which means being able to buy during a crisis when "everyone" wants to sell, and then hold out through the rough period until the market improves. How can you as an entrepreneur and business booster make sure you are **cash positive** at the right times? By doing so, you will be providing liquidity to illiquid markets, and that can be very valuable, especially if the seller has to sell.

Cryptocurrency is currently doing wonders for liquidity. Transactions that take days with the fiat system take seconds with cryptocurrency. Transaction costs are lowered, **speed of delivery increased**. There is a vast untapped potential for both cryptocurrencies and applications of the underlying **blockchain** technology, to dramatically influence the factors that shape the liquidity in many markets.

Will you be the entrepreneur that can harness those capabilities in your market? The combination of cryptocurrencies, blockchain technology and artificial intelligence applications will create big changes in many markets in the years to come. Truly, we can paraphrase Buzz Lightyear and say that in the near future, we are headed "To liquidity and beyond!"

HEMISPHERE

THE MOVERS AND SHAKERS
ON THE SKIES OF THE WORLD

By Christian Bartsch

The new Cessna Citation Hemisphere offers frequent inter continent travelers a great flight experience.

Cessna has opened up a new level of quality in the business class jets world. As you settle into seats designed for maximum comfort, over-sized windows let natural light fill the cabin. Three individual zones are equally well-suited for moving your business forward or affording a relaxing environment between your destinations. The Hemisphere will incorporate a full fly-by-wire flight control system, providing the latest-design for superior performance.

Time-saving speed. Ambitious range. Low cabin altitude. Modern additive manufacturing techniques.

The Cessna Citation Hemisphere is a 4500 nautical miles (=8300 km) range business jet with the widest cabin in its class. The maximum speed of Mach 0.9 is astonishing.

The Citation Hemisphere integrates a **new clean-sheet design**. The three-zone cabin offers a stand-up clearance of more than 6.2ft, while the maximum cabin altitude will be 5000ft.

The interior furnishings, including seats and cabinets, will be designed and handcrafted by Cessna in-house. The seats will be fully-berthable, and equipped with a thermo-electric technology, which provides better heating and cooling comfort for the passengers.

The integrated avionics system includes the SmartView Synthetic Vision System (SVS), which provides conformal **three-dimensional view of the runways**, terrain and obstacles, even in challenging weather conditions.

The Connected Aircraft solution aboard the aircraft offers satellite communications and connectivity airtime, as well as maintenance apps and services.

The aircraft's cockpit provides access to the IntuVue volumetric weather radar system.

For more information on the Citation Hemisphere please visit:

www.cessna.com

SITUATIONAL AWARENESS

Situational awareness and life lessons:
Living and working in Japan

By Louis Kotzé

Louis is a qualified journalist and editor with over ten years' experience in the field in editing, journalism and translation. He has been to Japan three times.

It was really a dream come true when I visited Japan for the first time, many years ago. But of all the wonderful things I experienced in Japan during that time, working for a newspaper in Tokyo was right at the top of my list of WOW things!

This was a chance for me to see one of the world's most developed countries with a wide array in technology and trading. Different sectors include Information Technology, Banking, Automotive, Engineering, Retail, Communications and Electronics.

Here some of the world's biggest companies and industries originated; big names such as Toyota, Suzuki, Mazda, Honda, Nissan, Subaru, Mitsubishi, Kia, Daihatsu, Isuzu, Yamaha, Sony, Canon, Fujifilm, Nikon, Panasonic, Hitachi, Bridgestone and Kenwood Electronics.

I had the privilege of visiting Toyota Motors – the largest company in Japan with a total revenue of 235 billion dollars – during my internship in Tokyo and interviewing two of

their managers about their exports to South Africa.

At this point, I was studying journalism at the *University of Port Elizabeth* (now NMMU) in South Africa to become a journalist. I did several internships during my honors degree, all over South Africa, but I managed to land an internship in Tokyo, Japan, at an English evening newspaper called **The Asahi Evening News**!

Not only was I about to discover the culture and language of Japan, something I knew very little about, but I was also going to get first-hand experience of the ins and outs of **the newspaper world** in Tokyo, and I was going to see places in the city I would never see otherwise. I could not wait to get started!

Then the day finally arrived. It was 5 o' clock in the morning when my alarm went off. I got out of bed and put on the kettle to make myself a strong cup of coffee or *kohii* as the Japanese say. Full of enthusiasm, I got ready for my first day of a two-month internship at *The Asahi Evening News*.

About an hour later, I got on my

bicycle, backpack on my back with everything I needed for the day, and off I went. It was already light outside as I cycled to the train station for the next part of my journey to the newspaper. I soon found the parking lot for my bicycle, where thousands of bicycles are parked every day – truly a sight to behold.

Then I grabbed the train, or *Yamanote Line*, which is a train that goes around Tokyo and stops at every station.

After about 20 minutes, I got off and tackled the last ten minutes of my journey to the newspaper on foot.

On my way to the office, I noticed that many advertisements alongside the road had celebrities in them.

"I later learned that the Japanese are absolutely crazy about celebrities in ads. I still remember one coffee ad with Brad Pitt where he ran up a hill, shouted something in Japanese, and then drank a cup of coffee!"

When I finally arrived, I was greeted by the editor and staff of the newspaper. After a few thorough introductions, they showed me that I can have breakfast there; either in the form of a Western breakfast, consisting of two buns, some jam and butter, or a proper Japanese breakfast with many wonderful and delicious surprises!

Of course, I chose the Japanese breakfast, and so finally my journey at the newspaper started.

My **first official interview** for the newspaper was with two managers for **Toyota Motors** about their exports to South Africa. This was quite daunting, as everything was really formal and I **had to know all the etiquette rules** beforehand. I had my own business card, or *meeshi* in Japanese even though I was an intern!

This is how important business cards are to the Japanese.

"I learned early on to always have a business card with me when I went for interviews; and it is always good to have one with you in Japan, whether you are a business person, journalist or entrepreneur. "

Another lesson I learned before my interview was that the Japanese do not shake hands traditionally like we do in South Africa (even though these days you do see that). Rather, they bow when greeting others.

Also, the more important a person is in Japan, the lower you bow. It became a habit of mine to bow to people there. It eventually forms part of your daily routine. I even bowed to greet people back in South Africa, long after my visit to Japan – sometimes to the amusement of others!

The last bit of advice my editor gave to me before my interview was this. **Do not rush the Japanese.** They take their time to make decisions and normally make a decision as a group.

So, **be patient** and you will get your answers. This is good advice for anyone wanting to do business in Japan.

Another place where you can see this in practice is in restaurants or sushi bars. Many times, when you are busy with a business deal, you talk about it in a restaurant where people take their time, eat slowly, think things over, and discuss it in a group. It may take a few hours before a decision is made.

"This is just how the Japanese do business. You have to earn their trust, relax with them, eat with them, and show them that they can trust you and do business with you."

A few weeks later into my internship, I went to do an interview with the owner of an African art gallery in Tokyo, and this turned out to become my **most exciting interview**. After a bit of a detour to find the place, I finally discovered the quaint little gallery, met the owner, bowed, and swopped out business cards.

We started to talk about his gallery and about Africa. Here I was in a country thousands of kilometers from home, in an African art gallery, and I felt like I was temporarily back home in South Africa. Art really is universal.

Then the owner told me he is also the director of an *African film festival*, and I decided to do a preview for the festival for the newspaper, which my boss back at the office later approved.

A few weeks later, I visited the art gallery again, and then discovered something truly interesting! One of the movies in the festival was a movie based on a *German book* which I did in German III at university the year before, and the people from the festival did not even know about the book! I therefore did an article for them on the similarities and differences between the movie and the book, something they really appreciated. It felt surreal that I could use information I learned in German class in Japan! It truly is a small world.

After many stories, adventures and getting lost in Tokyo a number of times, my final day at the newspaper finally arrived. I almost could not believe it was over. As a gesture from

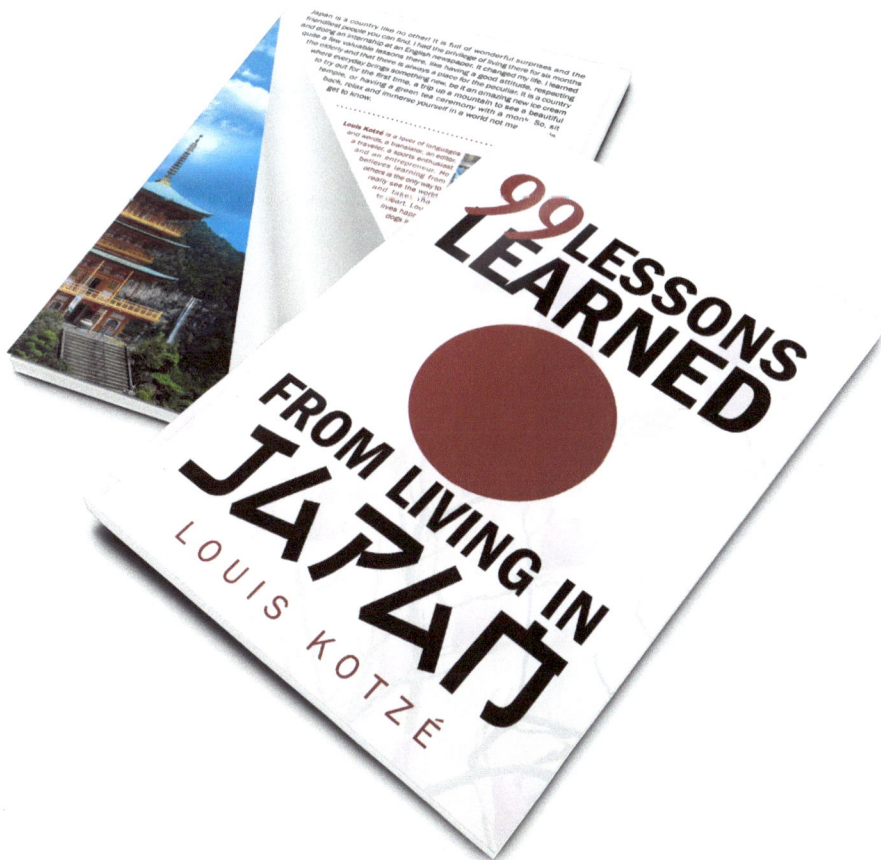

the managers at the newspaper, they *invited me for drinks* that evening to say goodbye and wish me well on my journey ahead. I have to be honest with you, there are few places in the world *where people are as kind,* friendly and warm than in Japan. It reminded to be the same towards others.

Anyway, that evening I sat down with the management of the newspaper (yes, it was a little daunting), but after a beer and some laughs, I started to relax. I thanked them for a wonderful, **once-in-a-lifetime chance** (even though my hair got a little greyer during my internship!) to be part of such a wonderful team.

One thing you can say about the Japanese is this: They work very, very hard, but they relax just as much! The Japanese workforce is well-known for their **excellent work ethics and high levels of productivity**, and at the same time creating excellent quality work.

They have a long history of recovering from historic events such as World War I and II, and always come out on top despite facing frequent natural disasters such as *earthquakes and tsunamis*. There are about **1 500 earthquakes** in Japan every year. I experienced a few of these myself, even one while I was in the office at the newspaper on the ninth floor with the building shaking from side to side. Luckily, in Japan the buildings are created to withstand earthquakes.

A month or so later, I experienced another part of Japanese culture. My father was invited to visit a work colleague of him. We went to their house, and there we had to take off our shoes, and put on special slippers to wear in the house. Other than the fact that this helps to keep the house clean, it is also a symbol of respect.

"When you enter a business person's home to talk about a business deal, taking off your shoes is also as sign that you enter the home, and the conversation, with a clean, fresh mindset and that you have the utmost respect for the person you are talking to."

We also took gifts for my father's colleague and wife, as this is another part of Japanese etiquette. You always have to take a gift when someone invites you to their home in Japan, preferably wrapped as pretty as possible. Also, do not refuse any gift if offered to you, although objecting at first is a sign of good practice. However, just be careful not to tell your host how beautiful something in their home is, because they might just offer it to you as a gift, which could get a little awkward!

Working and living in Japan has really changed my life forever. I have learned so much during my time there, and still apply all those lessons, even today.

"As an aspiring entrepreneur myself, and regularly meeting new people from other cultures and languages, I keep reminding myself that there is always something I can learn from others, and to always be kind, gentle and understanding."

DIVERSIFY YOUR WEALTH

Keep your money working with a strategic, long-term and sustainable opportunity

Investing capital is becoming a painful experience for people with a diversified wealth.

Governments are constantly changing their tax and liberty rules. Crypto currency companies are being closed by authorities as they are perceived as threat to national security.

Those who have been more venturous in investing in ICOs and other crypto services have fallen prey to Internet scams run by non existent companies.

The business model, terms and opportunities were reviewed by the German financial authority (BaFin) in 2017. Eventually they classified it as a innovative

service that is non a financial product and therefore is not subject to regulatory rules and licenses within Germany.

Liberty is a kind of freedom that allows privacy to remain private to the extent you personally are willing to allow. As the OECD are binding more country to a new transparency regime, privateers and business people are having to experience scrutiny by authorities who have no level of wealth or business education.

Therefore they are unable to have the forward thinking of innovators and business leaders. People desire to have control over their destiny. Therefore they diversify their portfolio across a multitude of asset types.

Mine Your Wealth is designed to offer an easy entry into niche investment opportunities.

If you have above $100,000 to invest in medium to high risk opportunities, our team can help you get started without the pain of doing it all yourself.

As entrepreneurs know, even in business there is no 100% security for investing in the development of a new product or service. Company owners see every day the risks of doing business.

Therefore we prefer as clients those investors who have the mindset necessary to grow wealth applying a long-term perspective. Therefore successful people are not afraid of haters and non-believers who do not have the ability to be in the future.

If you believe you are ready to diversify your wealth, then come and join our clients from all continents. Let us have a personal conversation.

Mine Your Wealth

www.mineyourwealth.com

info@mineyourwealth.com

CONTINENTAL

THE MOVERS AND SHAKERS

By Christian Bartsch

The new Continental GT offers a luxurious opportunity to travel in elegance while combining it with a conservative touch of sportiveness.

The new Bentley Continental GT dedicates luxury in its bold sculptured way as no one other could have **designed, engineered and handcrafted** in Britain. If you are into an innovative mind set then you will adore this **innovative luxurious interior**. The interior designers have created their masterpiece in the Continental GT as they integrated

handcrafted natural material with cutting-edge technology.

This is the **third generation** of the Bentley Continental GT. The engineering and craftsmanship of the interior resembles the attention to detail involved in the creation of an all-new Bentley.

The new "**Diamond Knurling**"

design is available for the iconic Bullseye vents, bezels and other primary control rotaries and not only gives a finely faceted visual impact but serves to provide a precise technical feel when operating the controls.

The third generation of Continental GT features Bentley Dynamic Ride, an advanced 48-volt roll control system for optimum car control. The control system improves handling and ride comfort, as well as making the car feel lighter and more precise. This system instantly counteracts lateral

GT = LUXURY

ON THE ROADS OF THE WORLD

rolling forces when cornering and ensures maximum tyre-to-road contact to deliver class-leading ride comfort and **exceptional handling**.

Following significant reductions in key environmental areas, Bentley has become the first UK automotive manufacturer to be awarded the Carbon Trust Standards for carbon, water and waste respectively. The Crewe headquarters was the first UK automotive plant to achieve the internationally recognised ISO 14001 environmental and ISO 50001 energy management standards.

Bentley offers customers the very best cars in the world – with unsurpassed levels of luxury and performance. Their determination to enhance significantly fuel economy is reducing emissions and develops highly advanced, sustainable drive technologies for the future.

SPORTS LUXURY YACHT SUNBEAM 42.1

The Schöchl & Nissen Yacht Builder is renowned for its sportive cruisers. Their Sunbeam 42.1 is a sports luxury cruiser which offers great space and brightness in the cabin.

By Christian Bartsch

The Sunbeam 42.1 is designed for sailing with a short-handed crew, with friends or family. For maximum comfort the cockpit comes with a length of about 2.4 meter - one of the longest in the Central cockpit class.

Sustainable thinking and lasting value are the hallmarks of the SUNBEAM family business. The mission was to combine the best materials and perfect design. The high fiber content ensures the typical weight stability as with all SUNBEAM yachts. The proven ergonomics of the SUNBEAM Yachts follows in line with the boats class you can see all over the world.

With the Sunbeam 22 Schöchl built one of the most favourite cruisers which you will find at many lakes around Europe. Their fixed and mobile keels have allowed these boats to be seen on the coastline of northern and southern Europe. Some of these smaller boats are even moored in Brazil and Asia.

Easy & Stable

The easy handling and high stability in all wind situations are achieved by a high ballast weight, a delicate tuning of the hull and massive hull reinforcement. This boosts the costs on the one hand but on the other hand it guarantees coexisting safeness, security and performance. And it maintains the quality and long lasting durability.

The Philosophy

The fascination of exploring new avenues and the desire for adventure explain the special commitment of the family run business in the boat building field for over two generations. The enthusiasm for sailing also reflects in their philosophy:

the constant quest to achieve the "ideal product" – a yacht, in that *practical functions*, **aesthetically pleasing lines** and **sporty sailing qualities** are optimally united.

To remain true to this philosophy they set high quality expectations for SUNBEAM YACHTS. They give special attention to detail and quality in unreachable areas of their yachts, as clean workmanship in hidden areas says more about the quality of a yacht than everything else.

Lead due to Tradition

In **1838** the family Schöchl founded their joinery in Mattsee, which is *30 km north of Salzburg* (Austria). Since that time, the ambition is for the highest level of quality in wood manufacturing.

Over more than 170 years of experience in high quality production and more than 50 years continuous development in the planning, design and shaping of yachts has made them one of the **leading shipyards** in Europe.

For more details on Sunbeam yachts visit www.sunbeam.at or contact them at sunbeam@sunbeam.at

DAVID FABRICIUS

More than words:

Success is possible with a sustainable blueprint.

By Christian Bartsch

When you speak with David about his business, life and core values, you recognize in him the proven leader who is able to translate his experience into real world answers for ambitious people.

David's clients not only experience massive success in their financial activities but also an enjoyable return to a life that has time for happiness and family. People often suffer from discomforts due to an unbalanced way of conducting their business life.

David's approach makes him a game and life changer.

David will listen and ask questions. He understands a lot about business success and failure. He has seen storms and massive wealth in short cycles. That is why he can relate to what ambitious strivers and high achievers have to cope with on a daily basis.

He will ask you these powerful questions and make you reflect on you journey:

"What is the business you are in? What is the problem you solve? Who is your ideal client? Answer these questions and bring consistent wow experiences at the right price to your ideal clients and you will thrive."

David Fabricius is in the business of **making the process of building wealth simple and attainable**. He and his team provide an *affordable Ritz Carlton-like quality experience* to ambitious strivers and high achievers who are hungry to grow financially.

SUSTAINABLE SUCCESS

Those who want to brand, market, sell, lead and invest better will enjoy a sustainable success. They can build financial security. Thereby, they gain financial freedom and financial peace of mind for their families

David believes in the combination of success, health and social responsibility. Therefore his clients desire success but also enjoy the life they always dreamed about, and positively contribute to helping to make the world a better place for all.

At David Fabricius International LLC, they treat people with kindness, dignity and respect.

David stands for building wealth without destroying families, health and soul in the process. In short:

"Wealth with care, wisdom and balance."

SOLVE REAL PROBLEMS

They are into building profitable and conscious businesses that solve real problems and add massive value, investing in silver and gold and in income producing real estate. His clients think that flipping luxury watches and super cars can be a fun and profitable hobby once they have a solid base in real estate first.

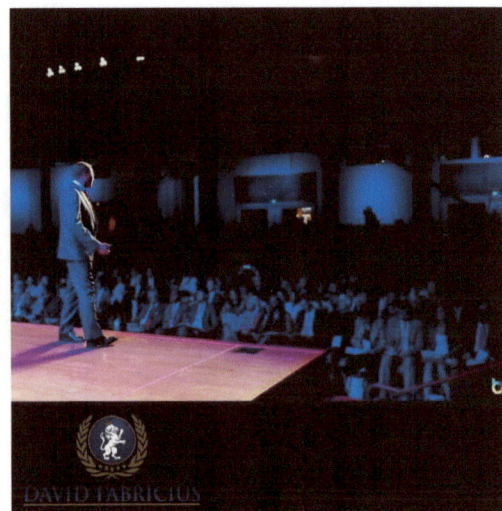

> *"David Fabricius gives leaders the courage to overcome hesitation."*
> *— Ariel S. Goekmen, Head, Cantrade Private Bank, UBS, Zurich, Switzerland*

David has a lot to offer. Not only his experience as an elite soldier!

UNBEATABLE PASSION

David wasn't always like that. During his childhood in South Africa he had to endure the discomfort of being unfairly assigned to be one of the members of the sick, lame and lazy squad.

His pure determination enabled him to break out of that spiral and thrive towards achieving what others believed he would never be capable to do.

He took up a desire to educate himself beyond the average what the school system had to offer. He did not leave it at that.

Being labeled as sick and lame, he broke out of that stigma and became highly competitive in the field of Karate.

UNBEATABLE LEADERSHIP

True leadership strength is not showy, loud and boastful. It is quiet. It leads with contribution and service, not fear, intimidation and humiliation. It does not destroy, it uplifts, celebrates and honours.

Save your destructive power for the real enemy, not people who love, follow and support you - it is the wise choice. It is what the wise kings and queens do.

LEARN FROM OTHERS

The more power we have and the more capable we are in yielding the *"life-taking"* sword, the greater our duty to choose the *"life-giving"* sword to be kind, forgiving and helpful to others. David learned this from the headmaster of a great Samurai arts.

Differentiate between real war and business, between war and civilian life. This is important!

David makes us recognize that doing business as battle is destructive. The book *"The Art of War"* by **Sun Tzu** is worth studying and yes it works but constantly being on the war path will always cause pain and losses on both sides.

Let's plant your flag on higher ground and expand your kingdom but let's do it with love.

Good and discerning people come for the love and stay for the love, not for drama and not for ridicule and oppression. Love!

ON STAGE

When you experience David Fabricius on stage he motivates and empowers your soul.

He fascinates you and you gain a new source of positivity. He is not about dancing around or singing silly songs. He is about true life and how you will build your wealth as a sustainable daily activity that has room for living

Just think about this:

> *How well you treat people with less power and wealth than you, and how well you get along with other kings and queens will tell you a lot about yourself.*

> *Even if you are blind to your own shortcomings, others are not.*

> *David truly loves to serve and uplift you.*

If you are sick and tired of struggling financially then it is time to act.

When you take action you do it with the right framework and relationships.

PLAN THE FUTURE

If you would love to be part of a **global community of like-hearted people** then you will recognize that David has a plan for you.

He is not scattered all over the place. He takes you by the hand and shows you the valley beyond your current situation.

David helps you find your why so you are able to have a blueprint that will guide you on your personal journey to greater success.

Yes, David will provide you with a **step-by-step and personalized day-by-day blueprint** to your first Million, 5 Million and 10 Million and coach you with the right amount of hand holding you need and want now.

He does not leave you in the dark without a compass and no hope.

MONEY EVENTS

He recently had one of his great **Money Events in Vegas**. That is where you meet fantastic people to network and gain insights into perspectives that prove to you **wealth is possible**.

Is this opportunity only available to people in the US?

David recently stated:

> "*We are expanding and we are going global.*"

His Money Events are attended by people from the US, Canada, Australia, Europe, Africa and Asia.

They are very special people.

Their positive attitudes and desire to grow by a sustainable approach unites them. Yes, they are about results.

Results are profitability, wealth, happiness, family, love and gaining wisdom from what this place we live in has to offer.

You only gain results by taking action. Success is not built on sand or on a cliff looking onto the waves which are knocking off the foundations under that castle.

If you thrive for quick and unbalanced success, it will come and be gone as fast as it came to you. A get rich quickly strategy is a path to self destruction.

That is why long term wealth is built on a **solid framework** what will withstand any thunder and storms. No waves will knock your defenses to dust.

So what differentiates David from other coaches in the world?

He is not expecting you to kill yourself for a goal that will destroy all that you love.

David is an experienced motivational speaker who has spoken in front of some of the most successful groups of entrepreneurs.

Their success is built on long term perspectives they pass on from generation to generation. That is how entrepreneurial families have built empires that are still there after over 300 years.

So who is his ideal client?

David's ideal client is a successful entrepreneur, business owner, and real estate investor with an appetite for growth.

He and his team especially love helping women and young male lions in their 30's.

Is this you?

Then take action now!

Your future deserves the success to achieve your goals in life.

IT IS TIME TO TAKE ACTION

Contact David Fabricius and his team now.

Visit his website at **www.meetdavidfabricius.com**, **www.davidfabricius.com** or get in touch with him via email **david@davidfabricius.com**

Of course you can speed things up and call his office at **+1-702-606-5276**

PHOTOGRAPHY FOR SUCCESS

The Worlds #1 Image for Success package makes it easy for entrepreneurs to get high quality exposure.

By Christian Bartsch

Because so many entrepreneurs feel they are unable to portrait themselves at their best, they often hold back. They fear their lack of high quality photos and videos will make them look unprofessional.

This branding service will help you within a few weeks to get your highly personal and top quality shots which will turn your features into the best ever of yourself.

You can easily travel to our key locations where our VIP Photographer Gabor Dobos will make sure **your photos will be phenomenal**. Our **VIP Stylist Aldrin David Verburgt** can help upgrade your personality with the right haircut and makeup.

Unlike traditional branding programs you <u>do not have to search for a photographer</u> that might not deliver the quality that is needed for a printed magazine. Even an online magazine will highlight your personality and business with professional photos – beyond imagination. Besides that, our experts **can create for your branding videos** at highly representative locations.

Our branding services offer a variety of opportunities to improve the visibility of you:

• Photos of you on stage, at meetings, in studio or even in traveling situations. Those shots are valued way beyond $12,485.

• High quality Videos of your Biography with multiple camera shots. Their value starts at $49,549 and reaches astronomical $500,000

• Drone videos of locations or action scenes to boost the dynamics of your public profile will often excel at values of over $1.295.000.

• VIP Styling by the stylist who prepared Celebrities such as **Charlie Sheen** before stage. Depending on the different services a day with our styling authority will be valued way above $29,574.

COST OF VISIBILITY

The cost of successfully expanding your brand visibility?

Reconsider this:

What would it be worth for you to be so successfully branded that even before you launch a new product people want to buy it? Yes that is what we call brand insistence. This is what will drive your sales and make it much easier to refinance a new product or business idea?

From our experience, we used such high quality services to increase the power of our branding. It is not good to hassle around by taking snapshots with a $25 camera expecting to get the result that a professional VIP photographer has at hand.

That is why Business Booster today Magazine partnered up with Gabor Dobos, as you will receive high quality photography with our phenomenal deal. You do not need to go to a hairdresser to get a haircut that will mess up your 10 Star photos. We have created the easy and pain free solution to your branding needs. People will adore and **love your brand** for its professionalism.

VIP CONSULTATION

For more insights into the VIP Branding Service, please contact the VIP Service Team at:

vip@businessboostertoday.com

CONTROL YOUR WEALTH

Keep your wealth under control as every day someone will want what you have and will do what ever it takes to get it

Learn how Governments are constantly changing their tax and liberty rules.

The crypto currency industry is being cleaned as scams are loosing their sales funnel. Facebook has changed its advertising policies so that the crypto field no longer can openly advertise for their services and products.

Same situation applied to areas that have massively suffered from investment scams.

Therefore it becomes even more important to be well informed what is hot on the market and what at the right phase to invest before the crowds head towards it.

Learn from the experience of other investors on how to make use of the opportunities in the fields of mutual funds and venture capital.

Get access to tools made in Germany and used by investors who have a diversified venture capital portfolio of over $2,000,000.

Benchmark your investments while projecting the development of an individual investment.

Understand the whys of investing in niche opportunities because their longterm success is not always easy to evaluate.

Learn from examples where the investor purchased stocks and doubles his money in 4 months. Some special investments needed 5 years to triple their

returns so that the investor got a 300% return on his investment.

The strategies needed for investing in such niche opportunities require an ability to spread the risk. That is the best practice any investor should apply as part of his risk management approach.

If you believe you are ready to diversify your wealth, then come and join our clients from all continents.

Let us have a personal conversation and schedule a call via:

talk.mineyourwealth.com

or

info@mineyourwealth.com

Mine Your Wealth

For more information on what the education hub has to offer on investment and crypto online coaching programs have to offer please visit:

www.mineyourwealth.com

SKIN & HEALTH

Your skin and health are your wealth, and why that matters for you as an entrepreneur!

By Aldrin-David Verburgt

We all have heard or read, probably more than once, that protecting our skin from the sun is important. But do we actually protect our skin with a sunscreen on a regular basis?

Most of us only use it when we find us ourselves on a tropical island or on the beach on a very hot day. We all love the warm sun rays touching our skin. Although culturally it is diverse, most people actually like that beautiful bronzed skin or tanned look. Now you may ask, who cares and why should this matter to me as an entrepreneur?

In our entrepreneurial journey we need to understand that investing in ourselves and our company is important. We do this to strengthen our position in the market and to grow our companies' success.

Do not forget that we as entrepreneurs are our own brands, we represent our company.

"In business looking good, healthy and well taken care of is a necessity, not a luxury."

What do we do to actually look good and feel good, to be healthy? What do we know about the skin?

The skin helps us to be aware of our surroundings, interact, feel and experience life and people, therefore understanding how the sun impacts us is key. Whether you are on stage performing or presenting to people, whether you are a coach and deal with business, your first impression will determine your success in business.

Did you know that the change of colour on our skin is a physiological process that happens within our skin? Due to the sunlight exposure our skin starts to form extra melanin D which causes the natural pigments in our skin to get darker. This is actually a natural protective mechanism of our body to protect itself. The more pigments we have naturally, the longer we are able to be exposed to sun rays.

Sunlight has several more good qualities. Sunlight is responsible for good mood, people are happier when the sun shines, the production of vitamin D is stimulated and it helps certain skin disorders like psoriasis and eczema to be more controllable and act up less severe compared to colder seasons or when exposed to more stress. Vitamin D is required in our body mainly for healthy bones and muscles and to support our immune system.

Unfortunately, this is far enough from the protection that we need.

Sunscreen protects your skin from the sun's ultraviolet, UV, rays. There are two types of UV rays, known as UVA and UVB, that trigger harmful changes in our skin. When we get sunburn, the top layers of the skin will usually heal themselves within days up to a week, depending on the severeness of the sunburn. The skin recovers from redness, sensitivity and pain but damage that has been done in deeper layers of our skin are permanent. This will result in premature skin-ageing. This is why everyone, regardless of the colour of the skin, should protect their skin by applying sunscreen. This is a recommendation by the Skin Cancer Foundation.

As an entrepreneur, your lifestyle is important, and when you have business meetings outside for lunch, make sure that you use sunscreen to protect your hands and face in particular. A good sunscreen needs to offer a broad spectrum of UVA and UVB protection with

preferably SPF 30 or higher and is water-resistant. Therefore, it is of great importance to use a broad-spectrum protection and at least an SPF 30 because this is the only tool to help us reduce the appearance of premature skin ageing and decrease the risk of skin cancer. Too much intense exposure to the sun, UV-radiation, will cause sunburn, early signs of ageing such as wrinkles, dark spots and the added risk of developing skin cancer.

"Radiant health is our new defined health!"

For example, both in the USA and in the Netherlands 1 out of 5 people will deal with skin cancer at some point. In Australia estimates are 2 out of 3 people will be diagnosed before the age of 70. Those rates are very high. Nowadays we have more knowledge and access to get the protection that we need for our skin.

This is why sunscreen is the most important skincare product during the summer, during a vacation or when living in a climate where there is sun all year round. We don't realise it, but we are exposed to UV-radiation all year round even when you live in four seasons. In the summer there's a different intensity than in winter. Even per day the intensity differs. The sun's radiation is the brightest between 12 and 3 o'clock in the afternoon. Ideally advice would be not to go sunbathing during that time.

Unfortunately, during springtime the most damage is done, specifically to our face and hands. That is the reason why premature ageing is visible first on our face and hands. Some even say that our hands reveal our true age. There's truth to that. Just like our face they are always exposed to sunlight and therefore also the UVA/B radiation. We dress ourselves from head to toe which automatically protect the covered body parts, except for the body parts that make up so much of our being and that we identify our unique selves with; face and hands. For women, due to fashion, their cleavage as well.

Truth to be told, we should absolutely enjoy the sun for all the good benefits but be careful and sometimes also be cautious.

It is all about protection of the skin! There will still be sun rays coming through. UV-B radiation will trigger the development of Melanin B in our skin, which we recognise as 'tanning'.

Needless to say that it is literally a 'Red Flag' when the skin turns red!

This is called sunburn, which means that we have been exposed to sun radiation for far too long. The skin's top layer, the epidermis feels dry, tight, itchy, is very sensitive and can be very painful depending on the severeness of the sunburn. Sometimes even signs of fever can occur. Therefore, this also limits your movability because of the skin's obvious discomfort.

Aloe Vera is one of nature's solutions to soothe and relief the skin when sunburnt.

In the dermis and hypodermis, the deeper skin layers, damage done by UV-A radiation has caused a disturbance in the cell production. This triggers premature ageing, pigmentation spots to develop and every time we get sunburnt it increases the chance of melanoma. Skin cancer risks increase as we age, which is likely due to accumulated exposure to UV-radiation.

Let us be good and protective over our skin, after all … it is our biggest organ of the body. None of us would feel comfortable when our skin is out of balance.

Looking professional and having a personalised look is very important to succeed, as is wearing the proper attire for the business occasion. A healthy-looking skin is equally important! Not just to understand our skin, our hair and how to take care of ourselves but to 'Dress our Face for Success', while staying the authentic

YOU!

In conducting business, we look each other straight in the eyes. On an unconscious level we pick up every sign of physical health and attractive behaviour and we interpret this as being successful. We all want to do business with a partner that's successful or has the potential to be successful so our business through collaboration can thrive. The very same thing we desire in our personal lives with whom we want to surround ourselves with!

There is so much more than meets the eye. Remember that our eyes and the skin of our face reveals everything about our physical health. Just like we want our business to be healthy and thus successful, so needs to be our physique.

"A Sound Mind in a Healthy Body Equals Success!"

As an entrepreneur we want to enhance our looks, dress well and use tools like make up that bring out the best in us, because we have been selling ourselves since the day we are born. Understand that when it comes to products for your skin, some brands offer special formulated foundations and sun powders to use specifically in the summer or during holidays or sunny tropical destinations. Not only for sunbathing during sunny days when we are outside most of the time but there are also specially formulated SPF's for daily use that are designed to use additionally of our skincare and hand creams with a SPF as well.

Even for hair there are special formulated products ranging from shampoo, masks, cremes, oils and sprays with a high protection formula to sensitive, long, coloured, chemically treated hair and even hair-extensions.

We can only make a good impression once … let's make it impeccable!

Let's make this radiant good impression last in our physique!

AT THE BOTTOM THE WORLD OF BUSINESS IS CROWDED!

HOW TO JV

Joint Venture Your Way To Property Wealth.

Building wealth, let us count the ways.

By John Stokoe

There are many ways to create a viable source of income, however you are limited when it comes to side-line income you can rely on while you pursue your other passions.

Investing in property is just one of the ways and has the potential to help you build wealth and maintain a balance in your life - spending time with family or interests while still pursuing your dreams.

However, a lot of people who are interested in property investing have second thoughts about it because of challenges involved with mortgages. Raising capital can be a challenge to some, but thankfully, there's a fantastic way to get you moving forward in the world of brick and mortar. This is by entering the world of Joint Ventures [JV.]

What Is A Joint Venture?

A Joint Venture is a collaboration of different individuals or entities on a project. Here, the collaborators are given more options in terms of skills, ideas and contacts and this opens opportunities with regards to capital.

With more capital, collaborators now have the spending power to be involved in bigger ticket projects so they can leverage and increase the value of their portfolio. Furthermore, the partners can split the benefits on the property taxes. Instead of paying for the whole property, all they need to do is pay their share.

Various JV Deal Structures

Even with a reduced risk profile of sharing the burden in a JV deal, there is still that possibility that you will encounter some financial hurdles.

Hang in there! We have outlined different JV structures to help you beat those financial hiccups you might face in the future.

Straight Joint Venture

Sweat vs. Money

This is a partnership where the other devotes all their energy - time, sweat, connections- in building the project. Meanwhile, the latter is in charge of taking care of the finances.

This can be a viable option for wannabe investors who have good connections but have some limitations on the financial aspect.

Intellectual Property JV

Knowledge vs Money

Do you know everything about property but are a little short on cash? You can use your expertise as leverage. Be visible and build your brand so you can share your knowledge to a broader spectrum of investors - Youtube,

Facebook, Traditional Media – and let people know about your know-how towards the subject.

Establishing yourself as an expert will make it easier for investors to trust you, which can result to them being willing to take care of the capital for the big projects you are eyeing.

In this business, it is always great to surround yourself with greatness. Learning more about a skill you are passionate about can attract the good energy, opening more doors for your business to grow.

Mortgage Host / Deed of Trust

Are you having trouble getting finance? Try looking for a mortgage host instead.

Just make sure that the deal is documented to keep the investor's and your assets protected. Pen a Deed of Trust outlining everything that should be declared. This can ease your investors' fears away, instead of going through a regular JV deal.

Tenants in Common Joint Venture

50/50

In this deal, both parties are on equal footing in terms of capital, time and sweat.

This can be the most effective option for a JV deal because both individuals/businesses are exerting equal time, effort and capital. Furthermore, this eliminates the possibility of future disagreements just because of the distribution of tasks.

1 For Me, 1 For You JV Deal

This is more of a give and take type of deal. On the first deal, you will look for the best project for you and your investor. Meanwhile, the investor will handle all the funding necessary for the project to commence.

For the next deal, you'll be tasked to look for a deal exclusively for the investor. Once done, he'll return the favour by funding your next deal.

In this kind of Joint Venture, both parties can still work on their own instead of being tied to a JV Deal for a long time. This arrangement also helps establish yourself as a trustworthy partner, minus the attachment that deals such as Straight JV, among others are composed of.

Chalk and Cheese

Skill vs. Skill

In this venture, you look for someone who have the skill sets you don't have -- it could be an investor, well-connected individual, who has an eye for properties that sell, among others.

As always, it is imperative that you build your skills -- you never know when you can use this as leverage.

Roll up JV

In the Roll-up JV, you ask for funding from a private investor with a percentage of interest per month.

Once you've invested the funds in a property, you should be able to pay your dues. In this deal, you are tasked to pay the interest 'rolled up' to the terms and time frame you've agreed upon with the private investor.

Where Can I Find All These Private Investors?

So now you have the knowledge, but can't seem to find someone who is willing to invest?

First, do your homework. Make sure you have a clear picture of the person you are looking for. Someone with money is just one factor, but it is essential that you share the same goals with them to avoid conflict that may arise in the future.

Once you've established a clear picture of the investor you are looking for, it's time to network like crazy!

Opportunities may appear everywhere. It may be family, charity balls, property networking events, millionaires' clubs, flying classes, launches, dating websites, you never know where you'll find them so make sure you are out there.

CRYPTO EXCHANGE

In the world of banking and trading the crypto currency exchanges are important.

By Christian Bartsch

When people travel around the world they usually have 3 things with them, which may be helpful. First of all, everybody will have their credit card with them. Then comes your local currency and that is accompanied by a small amount of foreign currency. International business is changing now ...

Some advocate of crypto currencies are that much enthusiastic that they call for the abolishment of banks. Even experienced traders are moving into the world of crypto currencies as they apply their FOREX knowledge to this new field of activities.

That is where crypto currency exchanges are **gaining considerable power in the market**. They are acting like regional and global hubs where people can swap Bitcoin for Zcash or USD or Monero.

Every new crypto currency that desires to be **listed in those exchange markets** has to pass considerable barriers. These barriers may be an entry payment, security checks, trading tests or a vast array of transparency documentation to **prevent any kind of fraud**.

In recent years exchanges have been hit by hacking. The uneducated media took advantage of this to exaggerate the true risks.

In reality more values are destroyed or lost because users do not take proper care of their **locally stored private keys** or paper wallets.

The amounts lost through hacking of exchanges are comparably low.

Therefore people are not so much endangered. Nevertheless, it puts up questions in regards to the user's behavior.

People need to apply reasonable security and risk mitigation strategies.

They should never exceed 10% high risk allocation in their wealth portfolio.

When you invest in high risk products you must be willing to **accept a 100% loss**.

Read the news on crypto currencies at www.MineYourWealth.com

BUSINESS CULTURE IN CHINA

Situational awareness and cultural understanding highly influence success.

By Janine Jakob

Most Western people seem to have the same kind of prejudices or first thoughts, when thinking about China. One of the first thoughts they have in mind about Chinese businesses or Chinese mentality is their culture of copying other companies' Intellectual Property or bad stories of failed joint ventures.

However, a lot of innovative global Chinese companies like Huawei or Baidu have been risen up in China the past years. Chinese and European/American cultures vary much from each other, therefore also business cultures.

Back to the roots, ethical codes by philosopher Confucius or Laozi can still be found in the way of doing business and behaving of Chinese people. Confucian ethical code consists of five constants which shall be followed by every member of society.

The five constants for example still influence the Chinese culture and business culture: benevolence, justice, proper rite, knowledge, and integrity. Moreover, it is followed by four virtues: loyalty, filial piety, contingency, and righteousness.

Many years ago, the lack of a juridical system in China led Chinese to pursue the ancient thinkers' values in life as well as business.

Whereas the Unites States was driven by values like freedom, American companies like Google give their employees much freedom in their working hours or the opportunity to do home office. Many Chinese companies, on the other hand, are still driven by survival and the goal to make a fortune to stop being poor. Some decades ago, the developing country was completely in poverty.

Now Chinese government plans to eradicate poverty by 2020. According to Statistics, in 2016, the year-over-year growth of millionaires in China accounted 10.7% with a total number of 1,340,000 Chinese millionaires.

People working for instance in Shanghai bring various cultural backgrounds with them, as they originally moved from different Chinese provinces or even abroad.

They relocate to the big cities for better education as well as better job opportunities to feed their families back home, and also try hard to provide their children better lives by investing all their money in their education like learning English.

You can slowly see Chinese companies like Alibaba Group in Hangzhou or also corporates or international companies in Shanghai for example providing well-being opportunities like financial support of gym memberships, or provision of meditation or yoga rooms in co-working spaces. However, this is also influenced by Western trends.

Coming back to the situation of still many Chinese people, they have a financial pressure to get a good job in a bank or a company, take care of their families, for men to buy an apartment in order to be able to find a wife to marry, parents' pressure to marry in their 20s, get children, pay off their apartment, provide your children good education, etc.

Looking at Maslow's hierarchy of needs, many Chinese companies focus their business culture on the minimum in order to provide their employees with the basic needs. Whereas in developed countries like the U.S., the focus is rather on the upper needs like self-actualization, as people do not need to fight for the basic physiological and safety needs.

Speaking with a variety of employees at different branches of Alibaba Group like Taobao or AliCloud, it was interesting to understand the employees' daily pressures and why many employees do not take advantage of the provided courses related to the science of happiness, meditation, holiday days, or the sponsored vacation to Thailand, but continue working.

A Senior HR Manager of the international headquarter in Hangzhou, for example, described her work life as this: She worked not only during the week, but also often during the weekend. Twice a month, she provided a training to customers which resulted in a working day from 8am until 2am. This training also had to be prepared with a similar working time.

Chinese mentality shows the wish for immediate response to WeChat messages or emails. As her customers needed feedback to their homework in the late evening, after finishing work in the office, she had to go back to her laptop at home around 10 or 11pm, to give feedback to her clients' homework.

Nevertheless, according to her, the hard work pays off and is worth it, once she receives her manager's recognition and attention. Eventually she was rewarded with a hóng bao, a typical Chinese red envelope with a money bonus, which she would then spend with her team on having dinner. Eventually she was lucky because a few Chinese Yuan were left for her.

Managers from various international companies in Suzhou reported, once they implemented more benefits and flexibility in the employees' workplace, they could see the trend of a growing laziness. This provided them with a new challenge and the counter-effect of what they wanted to achieve.

Achieving happiness at work or satisfied employees, is not a company's main target in China. Keeping harmony and good relationships with co-workers or family members is more important, as well as keeping your face even if you disagree with your manager which a normal Chinese would not express in front of everyone else.

Money is still a big driver and motivation for most Chinese people. Nevertheless, you cannot generalize peoples' needs and business cultures of companies in the developed Eastern part of China with the less developed Western part.

Keeping these factors in mind as well as ethical codes of Confucius and Laozi, you can describe different types of business cultures in China and compare different criteria with business cultures of developed countries.

SELF-ESTEEM

Let's talk Self-Esteem

By Marina Kotzé

In short, self-esteem comes down to how a person feels about him- or herself, based on his or her subjective evaluation of his or her own worth.

Thus, a person who feels worthy will feel good about him- or herself and this healthy self-esteem will contribute towards other attributes in a person's life, such as feeling confident in his or her own abilities and with a healthy dose of confidence, a person feels ready to face the world and achieve certain goals. Self-esteem may then be described as the level of *confidence* and *satisfaction* in oneself, resulting somewhere on a spectrum between high or low self-esteem.

As an occupational therapist working in the specialized clinical field of adult psychiatry, I can confirm the vital importance of developing and maintaining a healthy self-esteem. I often see the effects of a low self-esteem in a client's life and how it negatively impacts on a person's general health and wellbeing. People often question their ability or inability to amass to certain life ideals, and very often poor self-esteem is at the centre of the problem.

"Self-awareness is at the core of developing a good self-esteem.

Emphasis is placed on developing, as this implies that self-esteem is an attainable skill that is very much within reach for all of us."

Personally, my own self-awareness has made me realise that I want more value from life in terms of my career. Starting my entrepreneurial journey made me feel excited about new doors opening and a whole new world full of possibilities that I may access. The prospect of being freed from being stuck in a rut, made me feel good about starting my entrepreneurial endeavours after-hours. It gives me the courage and determination to continue working on my goals daily and to continue taking the necessary actions that will make the vision for my life a reality.

Without going into the details of the origin of self-esteem and how it is developed or not developed, the good news is that as adults with the ability to learn and adapt, we can acquire a certain skillset to ensure a healthy and functional self-esteem. And as mentioned, we can start at creating

self-awareness.

Self-awareness starts with our ability to take care of ourselves.

"As entrepreneurs and business owners or just any other busy person, it is easy to get overwhelmed with everyday responsibilities and in the process lose sight of the importance of keeping oneself emotionally and physically well. "

The importance of taking care of oneself cannot be emphasised enough. *Responsibility* may be explained as "response-ability", implying that all people need to have the "ability to respond" to difficult situations and challenges. Our ability to respond to daily challenges in a healthy way, where our general health and wellbeing are not placed at risk, is a good indicator towards *developing* a good self-esteem. Thus, the point I want to make here is that an intact self-esteem starts with appropriate selfcare.

The way you are able to take care of yourself is an accurate reflection of how you *feel* about yourself. Tackling daily responsibilities in such a way that enhances your health, and not to the detriment of your health and wellbeing, attributes towards building high self-esteem. I suggest you make a realistic list right now of ways you can effectively take care of yourself. Examples may include:

- Physical exercise

- Speak up for self

- Have enough hours of quality sleep every night

- Complete crossword puzzles

- Manicure nails

- Talk to a friend or supportive relationship

- Say "no"

- Allow others to take responsibility for themselves

As you are able to effectively take care of yourself, you will be much better equipped to also take care of other responsibilities as well.

The next step to increase our self-esteem, is to become knowledgeable of common self-esteem terms and their meanings.

Here is a list of some self-esteem terms and a brief description of each:

- **Value:** to regard highly; esteem

- **Leisure:** a time for nurturance through activities that are completed without rush or haste

- **Life-skills:** strategies, techniques, and tools to manage or balance day-to-day situations or challenges

- **Growth:** personal development

- **Assertive:** a learned communication style that is honest and direct

- **Independence:** freedom from influence, control or determination of another or others

- **Coping:** a behaviour that allows one to deal with or attempt to overcome problems, challenges, stressors, and difficult situations

- **Nurture:** to take care of and be good to oneself

- **Self-worth:** one's value as a person, as perceived by oneself

- **Forgiveness:** ability to give up resentment or desire to punish, or stop being angry

- **Self-management:** a balance of adequate coping skills, time-effectiveness, and self-control

- **Affirmation:** a positive, powerful self-statement concerning the ways in which one desires to think, feel, and/or believe

- **Well-being:** the state of being healthy emotionally, physically, socially, and spiritually

- **Self-confident:** awareness of oneself as an individual, and as a worthwhile person

- **Character:** moral strength; integrity

- **Body-image:** one's perception of one's own physical self

- **Respect:** to feel or show honour or esteem

- **Dignity:** pride and self-respect

Take the time to thoughtfully reflect on above descriptions and how it applies to your life. And when you do so, let me offer you to do the following 3 exercises for the next 7 days:

1. Make notes of ideas and thoughts that come to mind and digest these concepts.

2. Revisit your notes in days to come and re-evaluate your thinking process so far on self-esteem.

3. Envision your behaviours being impacted as a result of perhaps new insights gained.

You will be astonished of high much learning can take place in such a short amount of time.

Now, as your *understanding* of self-esteem has increased we will now focus on increasing our self-esteem. The end-goal is to have a healthy, functional high self-esteem. I will now introduce some ways and techniques to do just that:

1. People with high self-esteem not only talk and think positively about themselves, but also see the good in others and verbalize it often, focusing on *virtues, achievements,* and *positive adjectives.* Examples of speaking positively about others include "You're a very polite person", "You always look on the bright side of things", "You're a great friend", "The colour blue really looks great on you", "Thanks for being so sensitive to my feelings".

2. Recognize and bring attention to the *positive gains* you made on a daily and weekly basis. It is important to recognize and acknowledge your efforts and accomplishments on a regular basis. You can even write it down on a sticky note and place it on a wall as a frequent reminder. Examples of these are a goal accomplished, a compliment you received, a personal strength discovered or rediscovered, a new skill practiced, a new friend made, and a completed important task.

3. Present yourself in a *positive light.* The ability to acknowledge and present oneself in a positive light is a key to healthy self-esteem, as well as one's ability to establish and maintain friendships and business relationships.

4. *Acknowledge* and *accept* positive qualities about yourself. Acknowledging positive qualities in front of peers further augments one's self-esteem. Also, accept positive feedback from others. It is important to differentiate between a healthy self-esteem and over-confidence or arrogance.

5. Frequently remind yourself of your personal *motto* that you live by and hope to live by. A motto is a brief sentence or phrase used to state what one believes in. A motto that one values is a powerful way to strengthen self-esteem. Examples of mottos are "All for one and one for all", "One day at a time", "This too shall pass", and "There's always light at the end of the tunnel".

6. Create steps to greater self-appreciation and recognize symptoms of self-defeat. Self-esteem *boosters* are actions, thoughts, and ways that improve self-esteem. On the other hand,
 self-esteem *busters* are actions, thoughts, and ways that lower self-esteem.

7. *Positive affirmations:* affirmations can be a very powerful way of developing or restoring self-esteem. Affirmations are statements about a desired outcome as if it is already coming into reality. They are positive statements about who we really are. When we begin to recognize the negative messages we tell ourselves, we can then start to re-program them into positive messages by using positive affirmations like "I am lovable", "I can do anything I set my mind to", "I am smart", "I am strong enough to be who I am", "I will", "I matter", "I am big as I have to be", "My life is important", "I am creative", and "I do exist". Other ways to state affirmations are to start with "I accept…", "I have…", and "I feel…". Keep affirmations short and simple; choose only positive words; and make sure the affirmation fits <u>you</u> and expresses <u>your</u> desires. An affirmation is a gift to yourself – positive thoughts and messages produce positive results and behaviours. Furthermore, positive affirmations help diminish fears and self-doubts, improve self-confidence, and help you see the *real* you!

I trust that the information contained in this article has and will enhance your understanding and development of self-esteem. I furthermore wish you all the best on your journey towards growth and much fruit bearing success.

SUBSCRIBE NOW!

Successful people mind feed on a regular base! Get your monthly subscription of this international magazine.

Are you focused on growing your business? What drives you to succeed in today's world of uncertainty.

Entrepreneurship is a journey in life that will always be accompanied by uncertainty and challenges. If you keep learning from successful people in business you can make this journey a successful and trilling time.

Are you really a successful entrepreneur? Have you reached the level you want to reach?

! ENJOY OUR MAGAZINE EVERY MONTH !

Because some entrepreneurs are contributing to their local economies and that of other overseas communities, we created this magazine to **reach 20 million entrepreneurial** people around the world. This magazine will highlight many successful entrepreneurial activities around the world. As a truly global magazine we are providing **content to inspire and boost your own success**.

Unlike traditional magazines you **do not have to read articles** that were written by people **who are not in business.** You **do not repeatedly pay high prices each month** to keep reading stuff that will not empower, educate or even advance your life. Besides that, you get from us **access to a variety of additional guides** to help expand your branding activities, compared to what a mainstream printed magazine just can't provide.

Our monthly magazine subscription **offers great value** for your money:

- International Edition of printed Magazine (**valued at 67.00 USD**)
- Postage & Packing for worldwide shipment (**valued at 19.00 USD**)
- Access to our monthly branding guide (**valued at 1997.00 USD**)

Our magazines are printed locally in USA, Europe and Japan. All other regions (e.g. Australia, Brazil, Canada, Russia, Singapore, South Africa, Turkey, Zimbabwe) are supplied via our mailing service.

In order to purchase your subscription go to our subscription page:

www.businessboostertoday.com/subscriptions